BALAY: PETITE SUITE • KOEPKE: RUSTIC H[

T0069808

The Joy Of Woodwind Music

CD 3335

Flute

music minus one W.A.MOZART: ALLEGRO MOLTO, K.270 • A.KLUGHARDT: ANDANTE GRAZIOSO music minus one

W.A. MOZART: ANDANTE AND CONTREDANSE, K.213 HAYDN: MENUETTO AND TRIO one

C.P.E. BACH: ANDANTE • J.S. BACH: IN DULCI JUBILO music minus one

BEETHOVEN
Quintet
Opus 71

Printed in Canada

JOSEPH HAYDN
Minuet

W.A. MOZART
German Dance

JOSEPH HAYDN

Presto

B.M. COLOMER

Bourée

LEBEBVRE
Finale
Suite, Opus 57

ANTON REICHA
Woodwind Qintet in E♭
Opus 88, No. 2

© Copyright 1969 Music Minus One

MMO CD 3335

14

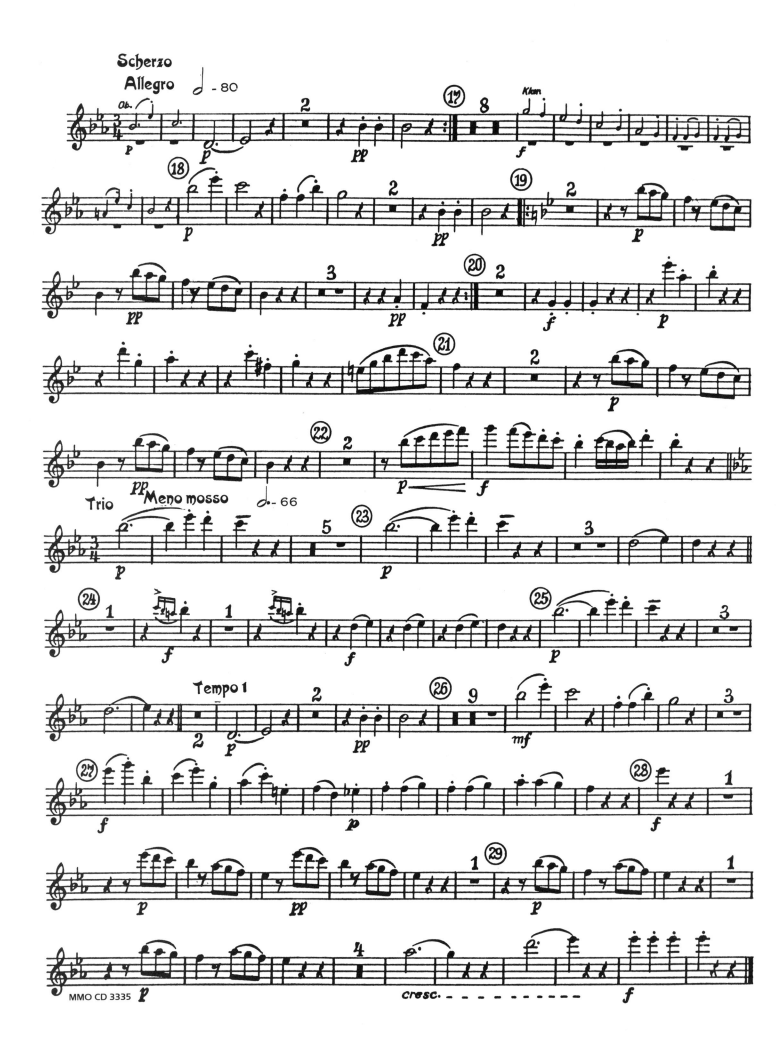

A. BARTHE

Passacaille

20

FRANZ JOSEPH HAYDN

Divertimento

4 taps precede music.

CHARLES LEFEBVRE

Suite For Wind Instruments

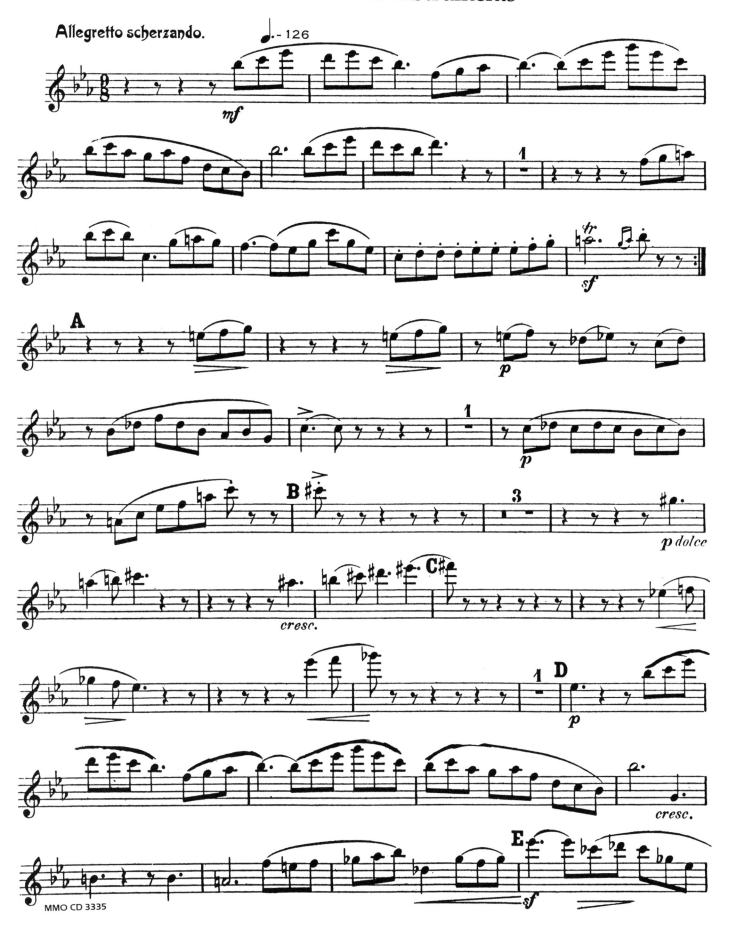

Trio Meno mosso ♩ = 108

(HOLD FOR 2 COUNTS)

MMO MUSIC GROUP, INC., 50 Executive Boulevard, Elmsford, NY 10523-1325